D1307291

INSIDE ANIMAL HOMES

Inside Bat Caves

Rosemary Jennings

PowerKiDS
press.

New York

Published in 2016 by The Rosen Publishing Group, Inc.
29 East 21st Street, New York, NY 10010

First Edition

Editor: Sarah Machajewski
Book Design: Mickey Harmon

Photo Credits: Cover, pp. 1 (bats), 17 Ivan Kuzmin/Shutterstock.com; cover, pp. 3, 4, 6, 8, 10, 12, 14, 16, 18, 20, 22–24 (rock texture) Juraj Kovac/Shutterstock.com; cover, pp. 1, 3–6, 8, 10, 12, 14–16, 18, 20, 22–24 (magnifying glass) tuulijumala/Shutterstock.com; p. 5 (inset) belizar/Shutterstock.com; p. 5 (main) rogelson/Shutterstock.com; p. 7 kajornyot/Shutterstock.com; p. 9 Wassana Mathipikhai/Shutterstock.com; p. 11 Gunter Ziesler/Photolibrary/Getty Images; p. 13 Gilbert S Grant/Science Source/Getty Images; p. 15 (main) Grigory Kubatyan/Shutterstock.com; p. 15 (inset) Ethan Daniels/Shutterstock.com; p. 19 Fred Bruemmer/Photolibrary/Getty Images; p. 21 Eduard Kyslynkyy/Shutterstock.com; p. 22 Sytilin Pavel/Shutterstock.com.

Cataloging-in-Publication Data

Jennings, Rosemary.
Inside bat caves / by Rosemary Jennings.
p. cm. — (Inside animal homes)
Includes index.
ISBN 978-1-4994-0871-3 (pbk.)
ISBN 978-1-4994-0884-3 (6 pack)
ISBN 978-1-4994-0913-0 (library binding)
1. Bats — Juvenile literature. 2. Bats — Habitat — Juvenile literature. I. Title.
QL737.C5 J466 2016
599.4—d23

Manufactured in the United States of America

CPSIA Compliance Information: Batch #WS15PK: For Further Information contact Rosen Publishing, New York, New York at 1-800-237-9932

Contents

Awake at Night

When nighttime falls and you go to sleep in your bed, one animal is waking up in a home that's much different from yours. Bats live in dark, damp places—places no person would ever want to live. Bats, however, choose this kind of **environment** because it helps them survive in the natural world.

Most people think of bats as creepy creatures that live in the darkness and shadows. Let's explore where and how bats live in order to learn more about them.

Is this bat home as creepy as it looks? Let's find out!

Flying Mammals

Bats are **mammals**. They're the only mammals in the world that can fly. There are more than 1,000 species, or kinds, of bats in the world. They're split into two groups. One group includes large bats that eat fruit or nectar. The other includes smaller bats that mostly eat bugs.

Bats are found all over the world, except for cold places such as the North and South Poles. The world's bat population is large, which makes these creatures very common.

THE INSIDE SCOOP

Some large bats feed on fruit. Others feed on nectar. This helps new plants grow by spreading seeds and **pollinating** flowers.

Large, fruit-eating bats, such as the one pictured here, are called "megabats" or "flying foxes." Small, bug-eating bats are called "microbats."

Bat Body

The first feature you may notice about a bat is its wings. Bat wings are made of bones and skin. The bones bend, which allows a bat to move its wings to fly. The skin that **stretches** over the bones creates a large surface that catches the wind.

A bat's body is covered in fur. It looks small compared to the wings. Bats also have short legs and claws on their feet. The claws are very strong and help bats do something they're known for—**clinging** to things.

THE INSIDE SCOOP

Bats from different family groups have different-looking faces.

Bat wings are more like human hands than they are like bird wings. The bones in a bat wing move like our fingers.

Where's the Roost?

Bats live in large groups called colonies. Some colonies have thousands or millions of members. The colony lives together in the same home, which is called a roost. Bats don't build their own home. Instead, they move into a **structure** that already exists.

Most people picture caves when they think of a bat home, but roosts can be anywhere. Bats have used caves, tree trunks, the undersides of bridges, cracks in large rocks, and even our own homes and barns as roosts.

This dark cave is the perfect spot for bats to live.

Hiding Out

Bats choose to roost in places that give them the best chance to survive. Bats are nocturnal, which means they sleep during the day and are active at night. Therefore, a roost must be a place that's dark, quiet, and out of the way of daytime activity.

Bats roost in places that are out of the way because it **protects** them from harm. Weasels, raccoons, and snakes are just some animals that **prey** on bats. However, if these predators can't reach the roost, bats can stay safe.

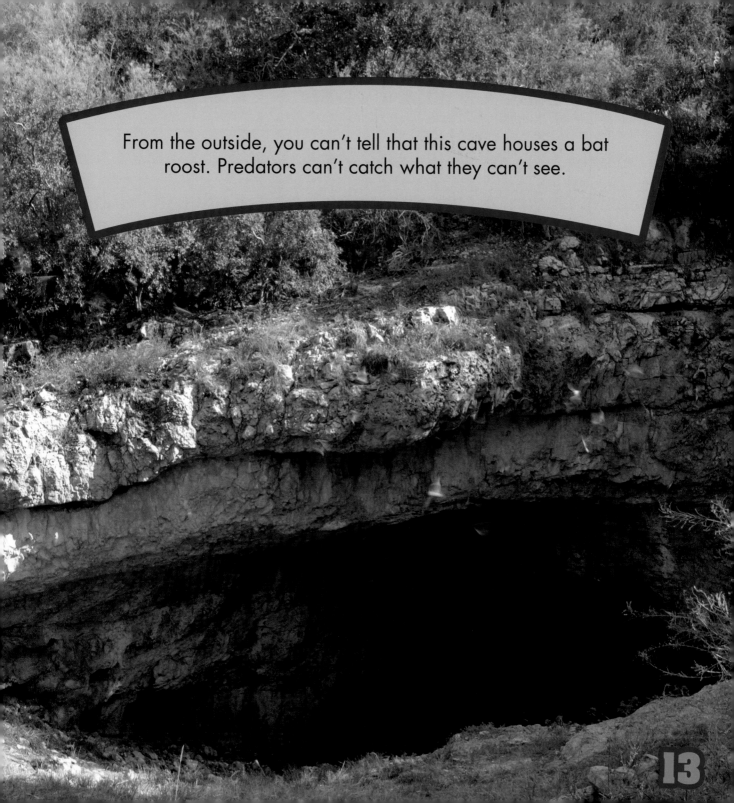

From the outside, you can't tell that this cave houses a bat roost. Predators can't catch what they can't see.

13

Upside Down

When bats are inside their roost, they're probably sleeping. During the day, the walls of a roost are lined with sleeping bats.

You may think bats look funny when they sleep. Bats sleep upside down. Some hang, and some cling to hard surfaces, such as cave walls or tree trunks, while sleeping. How do bats hang or cling all night without falling? The claws on their feet can grip things without using any **energy**, so their feet and legs don't get tired.

THE INSIDE SCOOP

Bats wrap their wings around their body as they sleep.

The walls in your home may be covered with pictures or art. The walls of a roost are covered with sleeping bats!

The Sounds of Hunting

After a full day of sleep, bats wake up and start a night of hunting. Megabats eat fruit or nectar. Microbats eat bugs. They find their dinner as they fly around the night skies.

It's hard for bats to see their food at night. How do they find it? They use **echolocation**. Bats make high-pitched noises as they fly. The noises bounce off of objects and return to the bat. The bat can tell how far away an object is and uses that to fly toward or away from it.

THE INSIDE SCOOP

The way the sound comes back to a bat tells it a lot about the object, such as its shape, size, and where it is.

Bats can make noises with their mouth or nose. This bat is using its mouth to make sounds that will help it hunt.

Bat Pups

The way bats live changes with the seasons. Their roost can change, too, based on what's happening in the colony. During the summer, female bats gather in their own roost to have babies. They like warm, dry places for these roosts.

Most bats have one baby a year, but some kinds have more. Baby bats are called pups. Mother bats stay with the pups for about a month before they return to the colony. However, if the roost is **disturbed**, mother bats may get scared and leave the pups too early.

This mother and pups hang out in a roost inside a cave in Indonesia.

Hibernation Roosts

Some bats hibernate, or go into a deep sleep, during winter. They need a home that's cool and won't be bothered. These roosts are called hibernation roosts. Hibernation roosts are often in places under the ground, such as caves.

Some bats don't hibernate at all. They leave cold places in the winter for warmer places. When those places get too hot, they'll leave for cooler places. Some bats return to the same roost every year. Others may find a new place to live.

Hibernating bats sleep close together to stay warm.

Bats Are Important!

At first, bats may seem like one of nature's creepiest creatures. However, they're also very important. Microbats help us because they control the bug population. Fruit bats help us by pollinating flowers or spreading seeds as they eat.

One way we can help bats is by letting them live in peace. Bats need their roosts to survive and stay safe. Most bats live in the wild, but if you find them in your attic, call an animal control worker. They know how to handle bats—and their homes—safely.

Glossary

cling: To hold on tightly.

disturb: To bother or interrupt the way something usually is.

echolocation: An animal's use of sound to find objects.

energy: The power to do work.

environment: Everything in the world that surrounds a living thing.

mammal: A warm-blooded animal that has a backbone and hair, breathes air, and feeds milk to its young.

pollinate: To carry pollen between plants in order to make new plants.

prey: To hunt and kill for food.

protect: To keep safe.

stretch: To make longer or wider without tearing or breaking.

structure: A building or other object.

Index

Websites

Due to the changing nature of Internet links, PowerKids Press has developed an online list of websites related to the subject of this book. This site is updated regularly. Please use this link to access the list: www.powerkidslinks.com/home/bats